IMPRESSIONS of
BRITAIN

Produced by AA Publishing

© AA Media Limited 2009

All rights reserved. No part of this publication may be reproduced, stored in
a retrieval system, or transmitted in any form or by any means – electronic,
photocopying, recording or otherwise – unless the written permission of the
publishers has been obtained beforehand.

Published by AA Publishing (a trading name of AA Media Limited, whose registered
office is Fanum House, Basing View,
Basingstoke, Hampshire RG21 4EA; registered number 06112600)

ISBN: 978-0-7495-6164-2
A04133

A CIP catalogue record for this book is available from the British Library.

The contents of this book are believed correct at the time of printing. Nevertheless,
the publishers cannot be held responsible for any errors, omissions or for changes in
the details given in this book or for the consequences of any reliance on the
information provided by the same. This does not affect your statutory rights.

Printed and bound in China by C & C Offset Printing Co. Ltd

Opposite: View of Harrison Stickle, the highest of the Langdale Pikes, from Great Langdale, Lake District National Park, Cumbria.

IMPRESSIONS *of*
BRITAIN

Picture Acknowledgements

The Automobile Association would like to thank the following photographers, companies
and picture libraries for their assistance in the preparation of this book.

Abbreviations for the picture credits are as follows: (t) top; (b) bottom; (l) left; (r) right; (c) centre; (AA) AA World Travel Library.

3 AA/T Mackie; 5 AA/M Jourdan; 7 AA/T Mackie; 8 AA/J Wood; 9 AA/D Hall; 10 AA/T Mackie; 11 AA/T Mackie; 12 AA/J Wood; 13 AA/S Day; 14 AA/M Moody; 15 AA/T Mackie; 16 AA/S Day; 17 AA/J Henderson; 18 AA/T Mackie; 19 AA/A Grierley; 20 AA/S Day; 21 AA/M Birkitt; 22 AA/M Kipling; 23 AA/D Tarn; 24 AA/S Day; 25 AA/R Coulam; 26 AA/A Burton; 27 AA/M Short; 28 AA/T Mackie; 29 AA/J Beazley; 30 AA/S Day; 31 AA/S Day; 32 AA/M Kipling; 33 AA/J Miller; 34 AA/T Mackie; 35 AA/J Wood; 36 AA/M Busselle; 37 AA/S Day; 38 AA/E Ellington; 39 AA/M Kipling; 40 AA/D Hall; 41 AA/C&A Molyneux; 42 AA/J Wood; 43 AA/J Henderson; 44 AA/W Voysey; 45 AA/T Mackie; 46 AA/T Mackie; 47 AA/S Day; 48 AA/M Taylor; 49 AA/S Day; 50 AA/M Kipling; 51 AA/C Jones; 52 AA/S Whitehorne; 53 AA/M Jourdan; 54 AA/S Whitehorne; 55 AA/T Mackie; 56 AA/S Day; 57 AA/I Burgum; 58 AA/D Hall; 59 AA/J Sparks; 60 AA/M Kipling; 61 AA/T Mackie; 62 AA/G Matthews; 63 AA/J Miller; 64 AA/M Alexander; 65 AA/A Burton; 66 AA/M Kipling; 67 AA/T Mackie; 68 AA/S Gibson; 69 AA/D Hall; 70 AA/A Burton; 71 AA/P Aithie; 72 AA/R Coulam; 73 AA/R Coulam; 74 AA/H Palmer; 75 AA/T Souter; 76 AA/J Henderson; 77 AA/I Burgum; 78 AA/S&O Mathews; 79 AA/A Burton; 80 AA/T Mackie; 81 AA/I Burgum; 82 AA/M Busselle; 83 AA/I Burgum; 84 AA/A Baker; 85 AA/J Henderson; 86 AA/D Forss; 87 AA/T Mackie; 88 AA/J Wood; 89 AA/S Whitehorne; 90 AA/D Noble; 91 AA/A Tryner; 92 AA/M Birkitt; 93 AA/P Sharpe; 94 AA/T Mackie; 95 AA/G Matthews; 96 AA/R Ireland; 97 AA/J Wood; 98 AA/S Whitehorne; 99 AA/T Mackie; 100 AA/J Henderson; 101 AA/D Croucher; 102 AA/S Day; 103 AA/J Henderson; 104 AA/S Anderson; 105 AA/E A Bowness; 106 AA/Tom Mackie; 107 AA/T Mackie; 108 AA/J Wood; 109 AA/S Day; 110 AA/D Croucher; 111 AA/H Palmer; 112 AA/S Day; 113 AA/G Matthews; 114 AA/S Day; 115 AA/J Wood; 116 AA/C Molyneux; 117 AA/F Stephenson; 118 S&O Mathews; 119 AA/M Kipling; 120 AA/S Day; 121 AA/S&O Mathews; 122 AA/A Burton; 123 AA/J Miller; 124 AA/T Mackie; 125 AA/S Day; 126 AA/T Mackie; 127 AA/D Forss; 128 AA/C Jones; 129 AA/C Jones; 130 AA/K Paterson; 131 AA/M Busselle; 132 AA/A Burton; 133 AA/A Burton; 134 AA/S Day; 135 AA/J Wood; 136 AA/J Henderson; 137 AA/A Burton; 138 AA/T Mackie; 139 AA/W Voysey; 140 AA/M Allwood-Coppin; 141 AA/J Henderson; 142 AA/T Mackie; 143 AA/T Mackie; 144 AA/A Burton; 145 A/A Baker; 146 AA/T Mackie; 147 AA/T Mackie; 148 AA/T Mackie; 149 AA/D Hall; 150 AA/S Day; 151 AA/I Burgum; 152 AA/C Jones; 153 AA/T Mackie; 154 AA/T Mackie; 155 AA/A J Hopkins; 156 AA/D Tarn; 157 AA/N Jenkins; 158 AA/A Burton; 159 AA/D Tarn; 160 AA/T Mackie; 161 AA/I Burgum; 162 AA/J Miller; 163 AA/M Kipling; 164 AA/N Hicks; 165 AA/S Day; 166 AA/J Miller; 167 AA/P Baker; 168 AA/T Mackie; 169 AA/S Whitehorne; 170 AA/J Miller; 171 AA/T Souter; 172 AA/T Mackie; 173 AA/D Croucher; 174 AA/N Hicks; 175 AA/T Mackie; 176 AA/T Mackie; 177 AA/R Newton; 178 AA/A Midgley; 179 AA/A Midgley; 180 AA/D Croucher; 181 AA/D Tarn; 182 AA/J Beazley; 183 AA/T Mackie; 184 AA/T Mackie; 185 AA/N Jenkins; 186 AA/S Whitehorne; 187 AA/A Burton; 188 AA/A Baker; 189 AA/H Williams; 190 AA/N Jenkins; 191 AA/D Forss.

Every effort has been made to trace the copyright holders, and we apologise in advance for any accidental errors.
We would be happy to apply any corrections in the following edition of this publication.

Opposite: View along Dorset's 'Pleistocene Coast' towards Portland from the cliffs above the dramatic rock arch of Durdle Door.

INTRODUCTION

Britain possesses a diversity of landscape that is unsurpassed; no country of comparable size in the world is richer in its patchwork of natural beauty. This scenic richness is a reflection of its wealth of history and architecture, and its people and customs. Just flick through the following pages and let the impressive images take you on a fascinating journey through Britain's beautiful and varied landscape. Every part of the country has its own special appeal and there's so much to see and do – choosing where to go is the hard part.

Scotland is one of the last great open space areas of Europe, famed for its moody Highland mountains, heather-covered hills, deep lochs and acres of tall green forests. It also harbours romantic castles, picturesque fishing ports, handsome towns and villages, and the splendid capital city of Edinburgh.

Fiercely independent, steeped in legend and grand historical relics, Wales offers an amazing variety of spectacular scenery. Explore the sweeping coasts of Ceredigion and Pembrokeshire, the sheer waterfalls and rocky splendours of Snowdonia, the high moorland swathes of the Brecon Beacons, and the gentle hills and wide plain along the Marches.

The North of England is rich in variety and contrasts, an area of huge industrial conurbations and of vast tracts of outstanding natural beauty. Within these pages are images that convey the best of this region: the wild and beautiful Yorkshire Dales and Moors, the magnificent Lake District, with its breathtaking mountains, sparkling lakes and grand walks, and the lonely and unspoilt Northumberland countryside is stunning. Lancashire's west coast has golden beaches and a mild climate, and Derbyshire is home to Britain's first National Park, the Peak District, where rivers cut through narrow dales.

Secluded East Anglia embraces the gentle, undulating hills of Suffolk, the flat and fertile farmland and wide skies of the Fenland, the unique, watery landscape of the Broads, and a spectacular coastline peppered with estuaries and creeks. Away from the urban sprawl of Birmingham and the Black Country, the Midland shires retain some beautiful countryside, from leafy Warwickshire with its fine castles, to the rolling farming country and mellow stone villages of Leicestershire and Rutland.

Close to the bustling metropolis of London, the south-east corner of England juts into the Channel; its marshes, wide beaches and high cliffs are backed by the rolling Sussex downs, the orchards of the Kentish Weald and the colourful heaths and wooded hills of Surrey. There is the New Forest, Britain's best loved woodland to explore, the enchanting Cotswolds to discover, magnificent cathedral cities like Canterbury and Winchester to visit, and mighty castles too, as at Windsor and Arundel.

The West Country is an area of great natural beauty, embracing the lush pastures and the high, wild moorland of Devon, Cornwall's rugged cliffs, the serene and rolling landscape of Dorset, and the flatness and huge skies of the Somerset Levels. It's a rich rural land, famed for its diverse landscape of upland moors, rolling hills and steep river valleys. Its warm climate and magnificent coastline make it Britain's most popular holiday destination.

Opposite: Lush meadows surround the village of Muker in glorious Swaledale, Yorkshire Dales National Park.

Rocky pinnacles face the Atlantic swell at Porth Moina, near Land's End, Cornwall.

The Iron Age hill fort at Uley Bury commands spectacular views over the Severn Valley in Gloucestershire.

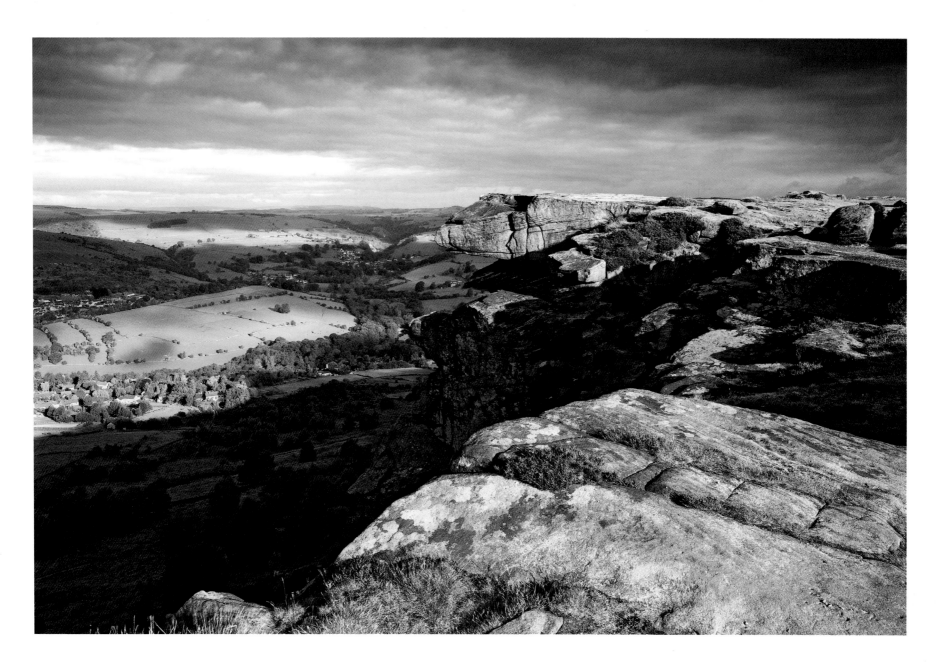

Curbar Edge offers testing challenges for rock climbers and spectacular Derwent Valley views,
Peak District National Park, Derbyshire.
Opposite: Pine trees reflecting in Buttermere on a frosty morning, Lake District National Park, Cumbria.

Looking across the sheltered bay to St Ives Head and its old fishermen's chapel, St Ives, Cornwall.

Flower borders in full bloom at Snowshill Manor Gardens (National Trust), Snowshill, Gloucestershire.

The placid lake at Ullswater is a picture of tranquillity, Lake District National Park, Cumbria.
Opposite: Bluebells carpet the woodland floor in Mill Wood, Hertfordshire.

Architect John Wood's magnificent parade of 18th-century townhouses in The Circus, Bath, Somerset.
Opposite: Buachaille Etive Beag reflected in Lochan na Fola, at the head of Glencoe, Scottish Highlands.

The Neolithic Lliwy burial chamber at Moelfre, Isle of Anglesey, North Wales.
Opposite: The last surviving Fenland drainage mill stands in Britain's oldest nature reserve,
Wicken Fen, Cambridgeshire.

A quintessentially English thatched stone cottage, Chipping Campden, Oxfordshire.

Windswept sand dunes and beach at Horsey Gap, Norfolk.

Kettleness headland from the Cleveland Way path, Runswick Bay, North York Moors National Park.
Opposite: Lush meadows and traditional stone barns in the distinctive landscape of Upper Wharfedale in the Yorkshire Dales National Park.

The Langdale Pikes form a distinctive skyline from Tarns Hows, near Hawkshead,
Lake District National Park, Cumbria.

A charming period shop front survives in modern-day Carlisle, Cumbria.

A pastoral summer scene in the Cotwolds, near Broughton Castle, Oxfordshire.
Opposite: The sun rises over sandy Boscombe beach near Bournemouth, Dorset.

Ivy and roses festoon a traditional stone cottage in Ashford-in-the-Water, Peak District National Park, Derbyshire.

The five peaks of the Cader Idris massif loom above Lake Gwernan, Snowdonia National Park, North Wales.

Steam train on the West Highland Railway crossing the 21-arched Glenfinnan Viaduct near Loch Shiel, Scottish Highlands.
Opposite: The Cotswold Way path leads to Painswick Beacon and a magnificent panorama across the south Cotswolds, Gloucestershire.

Pantiled buildings huddle round the inner harbour at Whitby, North Yorkshire.

Opposite: Sunset silhouetting ancient beech trees in Epping Forest, Essex.

The dramatic cliffs and pinnacles at Kinder Downfall, near Edale, Peak District National Park, Derbyshire.

Low tide in St Ives' harbour, Cornwall.

View along the beach and promenade from the pier at Eastbourne, East Sussex.

The medieval Town Bridge crosses the By Brook in Castle Combe, one of England's most picturesque villages, Wiltshire.

Impossibly romantic Eilean Donan Castle stands on a rocky promontory between three lochs – Long, Duish and Alsh – on the west coast of the Scottish Highlands.

Beck Isle Cottage and Thornton Beck, a much photographed corner of Thonton-le-Dale,
North York Moors National Park.

Bredon Hill in Worcestershire shows the Vale of Evesham in all its glory.

The River Usk and the Black Mountains, Brecon Beacons National Park, South Wales.

The River Fowey cascades through ancient oak and ash woodland at Golitha Falls, near Liskeard, Cornwall.

View across the golden sands at Colbackie and the Kyle of Tongue on the north coast of Sutherland, Scotland.

A thatched cottage at Swan Green, near Lyndhurst, New Forest National Park.
Opposite: A tranquil scene at Semer Water in Raydale, above Wensleydale, North Yorkshire National Park.

Timberwork on the 14th-century Little Hall at Lavenham, Suffolk, a town incomparably rich in medieval timber-framing.

The origins of the Devil's Chimney on Leckhampton Hill, Gloucestershire, have never been explained.

On the shore of Spey Bay, north of Fochabers, Grampian, Scotland.

A rainbow announces the arrival of rain off the Coniston Fells, near Hawkshead,
Lake District National Park, Cumbria.

Flat-topped Easterside Hill rises above beautiful Bilsdale, North York Moors National Park.

Britain's smallest house stands on the quayside in Conwy, North Wales.

A lily-covered lochan on Sutherland Moor, Argyll and Bute, Scotland.

A Dorset thatcher at work. England has more thatched buildings than anywhere else in Europe.

The topiary garden at Levens Hall in Cumbria has changed little since Guillaume Beaumont designed it in 1694.
Opposite: Pretty colour-washed houses line the harbour-side at Tobermory, Isle of Mull, Scotland.

View across Tenby's South Beach towards Giltar Point from St Catherine's Island, Pembrokeshire, South Wales.
Opposite: The crystal-clear River Eye flows through the pretty Cotswold village of Upper Slaughter, Gloucestershire.

Artisan bakery in the Cotswold town of Stow-on-the-Wold, Gloucestershire.
Opposite: Looking down the length of Loweswater to Mellbreak, Lake District National Park, Cumbria.

The half-cone summit and jagged cliff of Roseberry Topping, a distinctive hill in the North York Moors National Park.

The River Wye cascades over a weir in Monsal Dale, Peak District National Park, Derbyshire.

View of Abersoch, a former fishing village at the mouth of the River Soch, Lleyn Peninsula, North Wales.

Deckchairs line the promenade at Eastbourne, East Sussex.

Doorway detail at 12th-century Jedburgh Abbey, Scottish Borders.
Opposite: Sunset over Mudeford beach, near Christchurch, Dorset.

A narrow ginnel shelters a rose-covered cottage at Robin Hood's Bay, North York Moors National Park.
Opposite: View across the millpond towards Flatford Mill in East Bergholt, Suffolk.

Detail of the Cameron Memorial Fountain in the Charing Cross area of Glasgow, Scotland.
Opposite: Verdant summer scene in the Cotswolds, near Chedworth, Gloucestershire.

The 12th-century ruins of Dolbadarn Castle commands views over Llyn Pardarn, near Llanberis, Snowdonia National Park, North Wales.

Opposite: Heather, bracken and rolling heathland at Rockford Common, New Forest National Park, Hampshire.

Ivy-leaved toadflax flourishes in the stonework at Lanercost Priory, Brampton, Cumbria.
Opposite: The sparsely populated borderland beyond Bewcastle in Cumbria is one of the last unspoilt
areas in Britain.

Cricket on the green in the New Forest village of Swan Green, near Lyndhurst, Hampshire.
Opposite: A vine-covered Cotswold stone house in Bourton-on-the-Water, Gloucestershire.

The dramatic ruins of medieval Dunnotter Castle occupy an isolated promontory near Stonehaven,
Aberdeenshire, Scotland.

The River Glaslyn tumbles through the Glaslyn Gorge near Beddgelert, Snowdonia National Park, North Wales.

Looking out over the chalk cliffs towards the Needles from Headon Warren, Alum Bay, Isle of Wight.

The Beaulieu River flows idly through woodland near Ipley, north of Beaulieu,
New Forest National Park, Hampshire.

Clear waters below Birks Bridge over the River Duddon, Dunnerdale, Lake District National Park, Cumbria.
Opposite: View along the undeveloped coastline at Dinas Dinlle on the Lleyn Peninsula, Gwynedd, North Wales.

Rolling fields beneath the South Downs escarpment near Alfriston, East Sussex.

Pentre Ifan, a 5,000-year-old burial chamber near Newport, Pembrokeshire Coast National Park, South Wales.

Stone carving adorning one of the William Morris Memorial Cottages, Kelmscott, Gloucestershire.
Opposite: Lochs, moorland and mountain make up the stunning landscape in Glen Affric, north of Inverness,
Scottish Highlands.

Local gritstone cottages and attractive gardens near Matlock, Peak District National Park, Derbyshire.

Opposite: Sunset over Compton Bay, Isle of Wight.

The Callanish Standing Stones stand up to 15 feet (3m) high on the Isle of Lewis, Outer Hebrides, Scotland.
Opposite: A carpet of bluebells in woodland at Pendarves, near Camborne, Cornwall.

Cobbled Mermaid Street contains some of Rye's most venerable buildings, East Sussex.

View across Dovedale from the limestone peak of Thorpe Cloud, Peak District National Park, Derbyshire.

The green and knotty crags of Rannerdale Knotts spill out into Crummock Water, Lake District National Park, Cumbria.
Opposite: A striking, pink-washed cottage fronted by a traditional garden of rose and lavender in Shelton, Bedfordshire.

The market town of Wirksworth in Derbyshire.

Snowdonia peaks and the Caernarfon coast viewed from Newborough Warren, Isle of Anglesey, North Wales.

Dramatic cliffs at St Bride's Bay, Pembrokeshire Coast National Park, South Wales.

The vast biomes of the Eden Project are unique greenhouses set in a disused quarry near St Austell, Cornwall.

Corpach Basin is located at the southern end of the 60-mile Caledonian Canal in Fort William,
Scottish Highlands.

Boats moored along the River Stour in Dedham, Essex.

The ruined tower house and walled garden of 16th-century Edzell Castle, near Brechin, Angus, Scotland.

At 150 feet (46m) the falls of Pistyll Rhaeadr at Llanrhaeadr-ym-Mochnant in Powys are reputedly the highest in Wales.

Looking across Borrowdale to High Spy and Narrow Moor from Surprise View, near Ashness Bridge, Lake District National Park, Cumbria.

The ruins of Old St Peter's Kirk in Thurso on the north-west tip of Scotland.

Looking across bright yellow fields of oil seed rape in the Eden Valley, near Penrith, Cumbria.
Opposite: Rannoch Moor, a huge area of bog, rock and moorland, on the edge of Glen Coe, Scottish Highlands.

Windows peeping from beneath heavy thatch on a cottage in Madingley, Cambridgeshire.
Opposite: A misty morning over fields near Hawes, Wensleydale, Yorkshire Dales National Park.

Parson Hawker's hut on the coast path at Morwenstow, Cornwall.
Opposite: View across Loch Lomond to the Arroachar Alps, Argyll & Bute, Scotland.

Decorative ironwork on terraced houses in Cheltenham, Gloucestershire.
Opposite: Looking north from Foel Cynwch on the Precipice Walk, Snowdonia National Park, North Wales.

Autumn colour on the shores of Loch Katrine in the Trossachs, Scottish Highlands.

South Stack Lighthouse on Holy Island, Isle of Anglesey, North Wales.

Beautiful Hidcote Manor Garden near Chipping Campden, Gloucestershire.

The incoming tide races under the suspension bridge to Towan Island, Newquay, Cornwall.

Carreg Cennen Castle, near Llandeilo, Carmarthenshire, South Wales.
Opposite: Cotswold stone cottages in postcard-pretty Snowshill, Gloucestershire.

The famous striped cliffs rise above the beach at Hunstanton, Norfolk.
Opposite: Looking across the tiny harbour village of Staithes, North York Moors National Park.

Shafts of sunlight illuminate Black Mount on desolate Rannoch Moor, Scottish Highlands.

Pink-washed thatched cottages at Pleshey, Essex.

Rosy dawn glow over Bembridge Lifeboat pier, Isle of Wight.

Endless rolling views across the South Downs near Ditchling Beacon, East Sussex.

The lush green landscape around Ladybower Reservoir in the Upper Derwent Valley, Peak District National Park, Derbyshire.

Traditional Scotland: tartan and bagpipes at the Pitlochry Highland Games.

The walk to the summit of Mam Tor, Peak District National Park.

Looking across Freshwater Bay to Tennyson Down from thrift-covered cliffs at Freshwater, Isle of Wight.

The medieval Abbey and Roman Baths in the city of Bath, Somerset.

Looking across the Menai Strait and Thomas Telford's suspension bridge to Snowdonia from the Isle of Anglesey,
North Wales.

View across Edinburgh's Old Town to the city's famous castle from Calton Hill.

Groynes on Brighton beach, East Sussex.

The imposing twin-towered gatehouse of Carisbrooke Castle, Isle of Wight.

Rhododendrons line a pathway through the Rhinefield Ornamental Drive, near Brockenhurst,
New Forest National Park, Hampshire.

A glimpse of Whipsiderry beach, near Newquay, Cornwall.
Opposite: The 14th-century fan-vaulted cloisters at Gloucester Cathedral, Gloucestershire.

The jagged peaks of the Black Cuillins beyond the River Sligachan on the Isle of Skye, Scotland.
Opposite: Ober Water meanders through oak trees at Puttles Bridge, near Brockenhurst, New Forest National Park.

The impressive, high-domed ceiling of Ely Cathedral, Cambridgeshire.

Autumnal fungi on the woodland floor in the New Forest National Park, Hampshire.

The popular beauty spot of Betws-y-Coed, Snowdonia National Park, North Wales.

The rugged landscape of Glen Coe from the road pass, Scottish Highlands.

Colourful hanging baskets on a row of cottages in Grindleford, Peak District National Park, Derbyshire.

Opposite: The vast beach at Holkham Bay, part of the impressive Holkham Estate, Norfolk.

The ornate entrance to St Michael & All Angels Church in Lyndhurst, New Forest National Park.
Opposite: Woodland surrounds scenic Loch Ard in the Trossachs, Scottish Highlands.

Brightly-painted bathing huts on the beach at Southwold, Suffolk.

View of the famous striped cliffs at Hunstanton, Norfolk.

Springtime in a Cotswold wood.
Opposite: Scafell and Bow Fell dominate the skyline above the ruins of Hardknott Roman Fort, near Eskdale,
Lake District National Park, Cumbria.

The wonderful sands of Rhossili Beach on the Gower Peninsula, Swansea, South Wales.
Opposite: The River Colne meanders through lush meadows near Cassey Compton, Gloucestershire.

Surfers, bathers and families enjoy Porthmeor Beach, St Ives, Cornwall.

Opposite: A winter view across Windermere from Orrest Head, Lake District National Park, Cumbria.

Detail of a dry-stone wall, a familiar feature of the Yorkshire Dales National Park.

The River Wye flows through a steeply wooded valley on the Welsh border at Symonds Yat, Herefordshire.

Dent Head Viaduct on the Settle-to-Carlisle railway, near Dentdale, Cumbria.

Detail of medieval timber and plaster on Aberconwy House in Conwy, North Wales.

Thatched cottages leading up to Godshill church, Isle of Wight.

Field barns and dry-stone walls are typical features of Upper Wharfedale's landscape near Grassington, Yorkshire Dales National Park.

Colourful narrowboats on the Peak Forest Canal at Whaley Bridge, Peak District National Park, Derbyshire.

Terraced coal-miners' cottages in the Rhondda Valley, Mid Glamorgan, Wales.

West Wittering, one of the very few substantial sandy beaches in Sussex.

Looking into Danby Dale from the crags on Castleton Rigg, North York Moors National Park.

Sidmouth in east Devon was called by John Betjeman a 'feast of visual delight'.

A window in the wall of Claypots Castle, on the outskirts of Dundee, Scotland.

Haddon Hall viewed from the flower gardens, Bakewell, Peak District National Park, Derbyshire.
Opposite: Dutch-gabled houses above the beach huts at Bexhill, East Sussex.

A much-loved view of Skiddaw from Ashness Bridge, Watendlath, Lake District National Park, Cumbria.
Opposite: Wild Loch Shiel echoes with memories of Bonnie Prince Charlie at Glenfinnan, Scottish Highlands.

Bohemian chic: colourful Victorian houses in the trendy North Laine area of Brighton, East Sussex.
Opposite: Deckchairs on the beach at Sandown set against the picturesque backdrop of Culver Cliffs, Isle of Wight.

The wooded banks of Howden Reservoir in the Upper Derwent Valley, Peak District National Park, Derbyshire.

The River Meon flows through the timeless Hampshire village of East Meon.

Rose-covered cottage wall in Bossington, Exmoor National Park, Somerset.

View of snow-capped Skiddaw from the shore of Derwentwater on a perfectly still winter's day,
Lake District National Park, Cumbria.

Red post box set in a stone barn wall on the Isle of Anglesey, North Wales.
Opposite: Boats in the reed beds at Hickling Broad, Norfolk Broads National Park.

The Emperor Fountain in front of Chatsworth House, near Bakewell, Peak District National Park, Derbyshire.
Opposite: Stone path leading to the summit of Mam Tor and stunning Peak District views, near Castleton, Derbyshire.

Penygarreg Reservoir Dam, Elan Valley, Powys.
Opposite: The Strid, a treacherous rapid on the River Wharfe, near Bolton Abbey in Wharfedale,
Yorkshire Dales National Park.

The remote hamlet of Pilsbury in the Dove Valley, Peak District National Park, Derbyshire.

Graceful High Crag looms high above the frosty shore of Buttermere, Lake District National Park, Cumbria.

A glorious sunrise over the tidal River Blyth at Blythburgh, Suffolk.

On the Pembrokeshire coast path at Newgale, St Bride's Bay, South Wales.

The beautiful walled garden at Crathes Castle, south-west of Aberdeen, Scotland.
Opposite: A sea of pink heather covers Rockford Common, near Ringwood, New Forest National Park, Hampshire.

Looking through sunlit trees in Thetford Forest, Norfolk.
Opposite: The Roman Steps in Cwm Bychan, Beddgelert, Snowdonia National Park, North Wales.

Strumble Head Lighthouse on the Pembrokeshire coast, near Fishguard, South Wales.

A path through the beech woods near Burley, New Forest National Park, Hampshire.

INDEX